Green Apple

The American West

Told by Gina D. B. Clemen

CIDEB

Editors: Monika Marszewska, Elvira Poggi Repetto
Design: Nadia Maestri
Cover illustration: detail from "The Cowboy" by Frederic Remington, 1902
Illustrations: Alfredo Belli, Enzo Marciante, Barbara Nascimbeni

© 1998 Cideb Editrice, Genoa

First edition: May 1998

5   4   3   2   1

All rights reserved. No part of this book may be reproduced, stored in a retrieval system, or transmitted, in any form or by any means, electronic, mechanical, photocopying, recording or otherwise, without the written permission of the publisher.

We would be happy to receive your comments and suggestions, and give you any other information concerning our material.
Our address and fax number are:
Cideb Editrice – Piazza Garibaldi 11/2 – 16035 Rapallo (GE)
Fax 0185/230100 – e-mail: cidebedi@rapallo.newnetworks.it

PRINTED ON FREELIFE®FEDRIGONI

ISBN 88-7754-429-5

Printed in Italy by Litoprint, Genoa

Contents

	A Nation is Born	4
CHAPTER ONE	**The First Americans: The Indians**	8
	UNDERSTANDING THE TEXT	12
CHAPTER TWO	**Daniel Boone**	15
	UNDERSTANDING THE TEXT	17
CHAPTER THREE	**The Lewis and Clark Expedition**	20
	UNDERSTANDING THE TEXT	23
CHAPTER FOUR	**Let's go West!**	25
	UNDERSTANDING THE TEXT	30
CHAPTER FIVE	**Life on the Frontier**	34
	UNDERSTANDING THE TEXT	38
	Outlaws of the West	42
CHAPTER SIX	**The California Gold Rush**	46
	UNDERSTANDING THE TEXT	49
	Cowboys!	53
CHAPTER SEVEN	**The Indian Wars**	58
	UNDERSTANDING THE TEXT	62

A NATION IS BORN

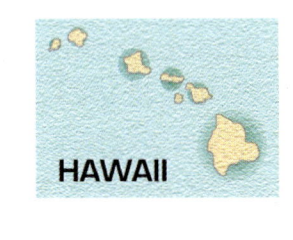

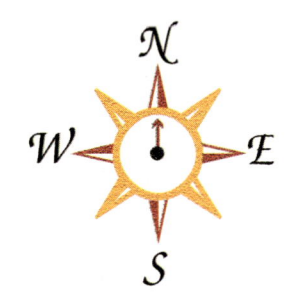

Population: about 250 million people
States: 50
Important Rivers: Mississippi and Missouri
Important Mountains: Rocky and Appalachian
Important Lakes: Superior, Michigan, Huron, Erie, Ontario

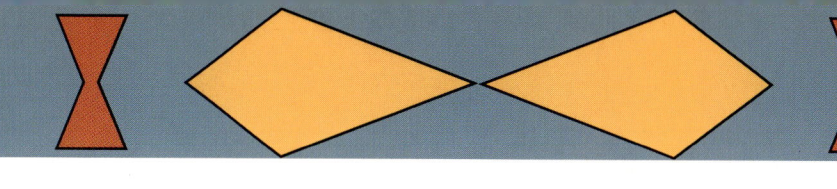

This is a map of the United States today. It is a big country with 50 states. [1]

The first European explorers came to America about 400 years ago. At that time America was an enormous wilderness [2] and Indians lived there.

America became independent from Britain in 1776. It became a nation and grew very quickly.

Enthusiastic people wanted to explore and live in the West. The story of the American West is exciting!

1 **Are these sentences true (T) or false (F)? Correct the false sentences.**

	T	F
a. The United States of America has 50 states.	✓	☐
b. The Mississippi and Appalachian are two important rivers.	☐	✓
c. America has four important lakes.	☐	✓
d. About 250 million people live in the United States.	✓	☐
e. The Rocky Mountains are in the West.	✓	☐
f. The first European explorers came to America about 300 years ago.	☐	✓
g. The story of the American West is exciting!	✓	☐

1. **states**: territories that have a name and their own laws.
2. **wilderness**: a place with no people or houses, where the land is not cultivated.

BEFORE READING

1 **Do you know these words?**

rifles

cattle

stagecoach

bow and arrow

tepee

sheep

tools

canoe

covered wagon

2 **Where is the American West? Use your pencil and colour in the part of America that you think is the West.**

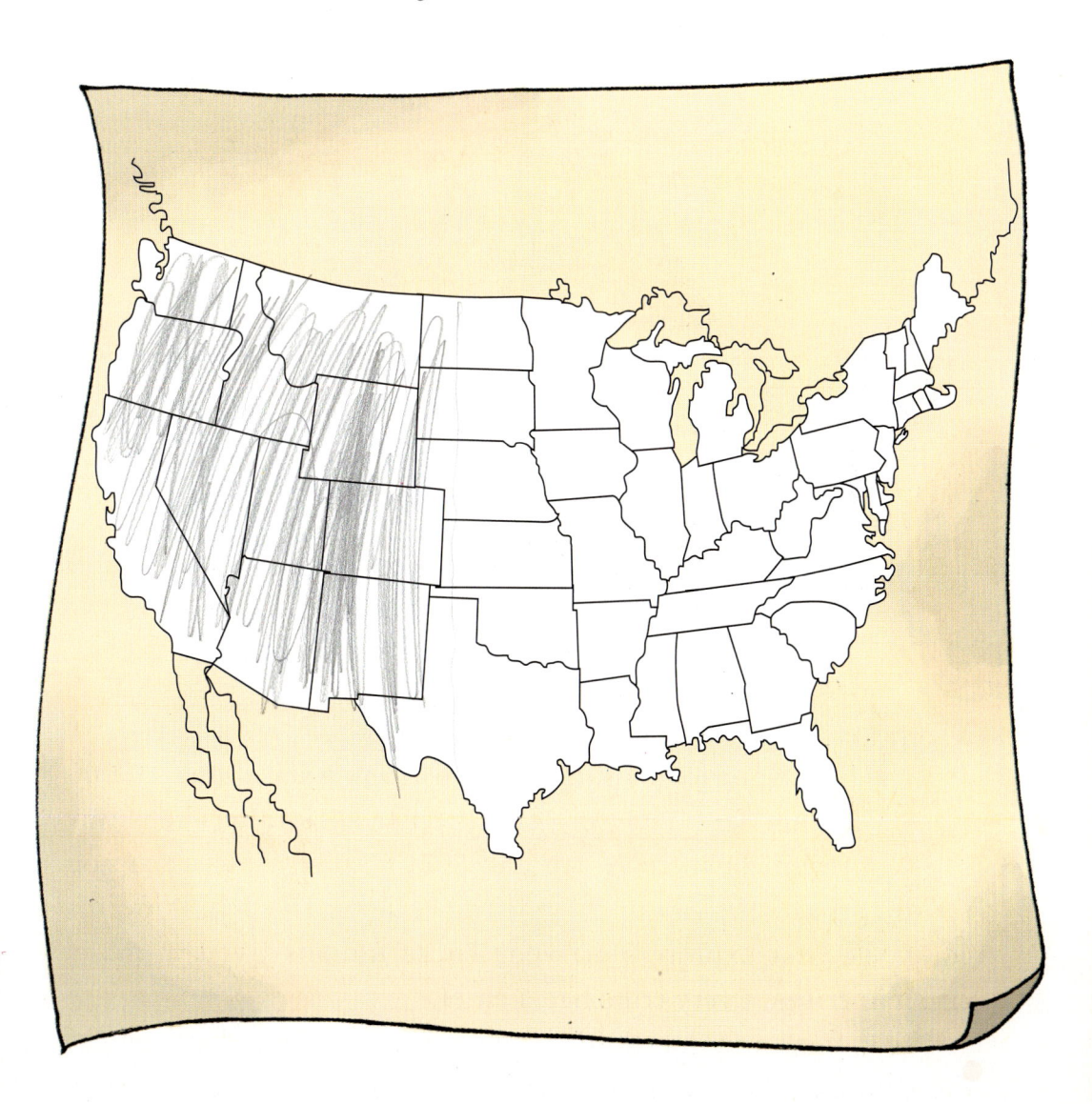

7

CHAPTER ONE

The First Americans: The Indians

The American Indians came from Asia about 40,000 years ago! They crossed the Bering Strait. Then they went down to North and South America. (see map on page 10) About 20 million Indians lived in America when the first explorers arrived. These Indians lived in many different tribes. Every tribe had a chief.

The Indians and the explorers were friends. The Indians taught the explorers how to grow corn,[1] potatoes and tobacco. They taught them how to travel by canoe in the wilderness.

The explorers brought the Indians rifles, tools, cattle and

1. **corn** :

Monument Valley, Arizona.

The American West

horses. The explorers also brought illnesses.[1] Many Indians died from these illnesses.

The Indians of the Plains[2] were expert hunters. They rode fast horses. They hunted the buffalo with bows and arrows or rifles.

These Indians followed the buffalo across the Plains. They used the buffalo for food, clothes and tepees.

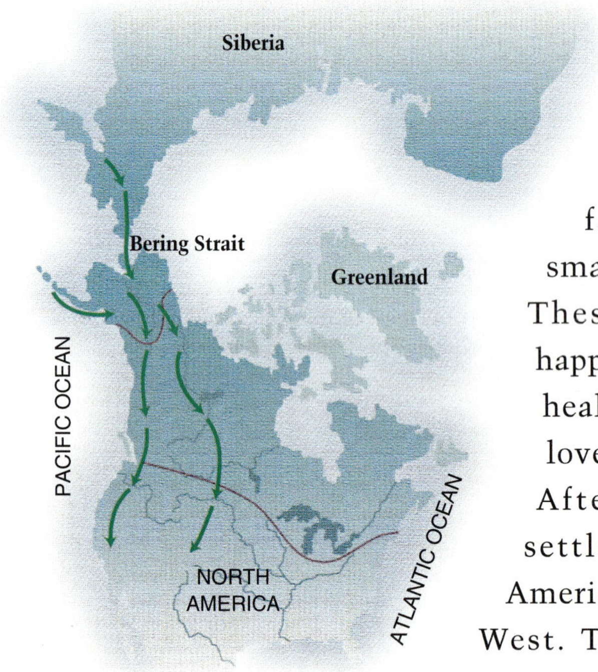

The other American Indians were farmers. They farmed, fished and hunted small animals.

These native Americans were happy people. They were strong, healthy[3] and courageous. They loved and respected nature.

After many years, more new settlers and explorers went to America. They wanted to go to the West. They wanted to live there.

---

1. **illnesses** (singular: illness) : when a person is not well he/she has an illness.
2. **Plains** : enormous piece of land with no hills and little vegetation.
3. **healthy** : in good physical condition.

The First Americans: The Indians

They took the land from the Indians. The Indians were very angry and the Indian wars started. Many people were killed.

The Indians lost their land and their way of life. They went to live on reservations.[1]

"The Dance of the Eagle" by George A. Catlin, 1830's.

1. **reservations** : government land for the Indians to live on.

UNDERSTANDING THE TEXT

1 **Choose the correct answer.**

a. The first Indians came from Asia about
- [ ] 4,000 years ago
- [x] 40,000 years ago
- [ ] 400 years ago

b. The Indians taught the explorers how to
- [x] hunt the buffalo
- [x] grow corn, potatoes and tobacco
- [ ] cure illnesses with herbs

c. The explorers brought the Indians
- [ ] new plants and herbs
- [ ] horses and buffalo
- [x] rifles, tools, cattle and horses

d. The Indians of the Plains
- [x] hunted the buffalo
- [ ] were farmers
- [ ] lived on Government reservations

e. The Indians used the buffalo for
- [ ] food only
- [x] food, clothes and tepees
- [ ] bows and arrows

f. When the settlers went to the West
- [ ] the Indians returned to Asia
- [ ] the Indians were happy
- [x] the Indians lost their land

2 **Climb the totem pole!**

INFINITIVE	PAST SIMPLE
lose	lost
take	took
want	wanted
love	loved
use	used
follow	borrowed
ride	rided road
die	died
bring	brought
teach	taught
am	was/were
have	had
live	lived
go	went
come	came

Start here and fill in the correct verb form.

3 **Use some of the verbs above to fill in the gaps.**

a. About 20 million Indians ...were... in America.
b. Every tribe ...had... a chief.
c. The Indians ...taught... the explorers how to grow corn.
d. The explorers ...brought... the Indians cattle and horses.
e. The Indians of the Plains ...had... fast horses.
f. The new settlers and explorers ...wanted... to go to the West.
g. The Indians ...lost... their land.

4 **Odd one out!**

Circle the word that doesn't belong to the group.

a. Asia   America   (the West)   Europe   Africa

b. Europeans   Indians   Americans   Italians   (settlers)

c. town   home   (tepee)   house   castle

d. sheep   (canoe)   cattle   buffalo   horses

e. courageous   strong   healthy   (chief)   happy

f. West   (down)   North   South   East

"Buffalo Chase" by Seth Eastman, 1868.

CHAPTER TWO

Daniel Boone

Before 1803 most of America was a wilderness. There were no maps and no roads.

Daniel Boone was a famous explorer and pioneer. In 1769 he travelled across the Appalachian Mountains to Kentucky. He opened the road to the West.

Daniel Boone and his family built a cabin and a fort in Kentucky. Boone had many adventures with the Indians. The Indians captured and killed two of his sons. In 1778 Boone was captured by the Shawnee Indians. He was their prisoner but these Indians respected him. He was a strong fighter and a courageous man.

Boone helped the pioneers. His fort protected settlers during Indian attacks. Boone was an American free spirit. He loved freedom and adventure. In 1799 he went to Missouri. He said to his friends, "There are too many people here. I'm going to the West!" America grew very quickly.

The American West

Johnny Appleseed was another American pioneer. In the 1800's he planted apple trees on the frontier. He helped the settlers in Ohio and Indiana.

Look at this table:

THE RAPID GROWTH OF AMERICA

YEAR	POPULATION
1781*	3 million
1819	9.3 million
1849	22 million
1869	39 million

*at the end of the American Revolution

"Daniel Boone Escorting Settlers Through the Cumberland Gap" by George Caleb Bingham, 1852.

UNDERSTANDING THE TEXT

1 Fill in the gaps with the words in the fort.

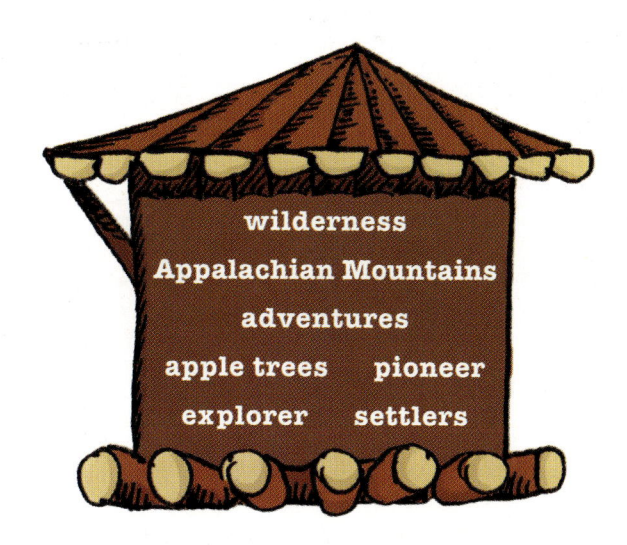

> wilderness
> Appalachian Mountains
> adventures
> apple trees   pioneer
> explorer   settlers

a. Before 1803 most of America was a *wilderness*.
b. Daniel Boone was a famous *explorer* and *pioneer*.
c. He travelled across the *Appalachian M*.
d. Boone had many *adventures* with the Indians.
e. Boone's fort protected *settlers* during Indian attacks.
f. Johnny Appleseed planted *apple trees* on the frontier.

How many people lived in America in 1781? *3 million*
How many people lived in America in 1849? *22 million*

2 **What time is it?**
Draw the times on the clocks.

half past eight   midday   quarter past eleven

twenty to three   five past six   ten to twelve

Write the times shown on the clocks.

20 P Six   11 a.P. Nine   5 to eight

4 to Nine   25 past 1   Mar 6

What preposition is used to talk about the time? ...at....
Use that preposition in this sentence.

Daniel Boone had dinner ...at...... 7 p.m.

Write a sentence using the preposition *at*.

Riding at five

3 Word search
Look at the places on the map on page 4. Then look below and circle:

a. two important American rivers
b. two important American mountains
c. one important American lake

M	F	P	X	C	U	O	H	Y	D	U	R	J	F
M	I	S	S	O	U	R	I	I	D	A	Q	L	G
B	E	G	U	T	J	D	C	X	J	H	L	Q	S
G	A	P	P	A	L	A	C	H	I	A	N	R	C
J	T	K	E	F	G	E	A	P	K	G	X	T	D
E	G	T	R	T	F	X	F	R	E	A	P	S	S
A	V	M	I	S	S	I	S	S	I	P	P	I	H
X	F	R	O	A	R	H	C	X	N	M	O	A	D
O	H	A	R	O	C	K	Y	M	O	A	D	N	K
Y	W	S	Q	O	C	T	O	E	C	J	W	A	Z

4 Dictation
Listen to the dictation carefully. Then listen to it again and fill in the gaps with the words you hear.

Daniel Boone was a famous pioneer. He opened the ...road... to the West. He built a cabin and a ...fort... in Kentucky. Boone always helped the pioneers. He ...loved... freedom and adventure. He was an American ...free... spirit. In 1799 he ...went... to Missouri. He said to his friends, "There are too ...many... people here. I'm going to the ...West...!"

19

CHAPTER THREE

The Lewis and Clark Expedition

In 1803 the United States President, Thomas Jefferson, bought the Louisiana territory from France. He paid $15 million for this immense piece of land.

President Jefferson liked science. It was very interesting. He wanted to learn about the plants and animals of the new territory.

In May 1804 President Jefferson asked Meriwether Lewis and William Clark to explore the Louisiana Purchase.[1] Lewis and Clark were the first white men to see this land.

This important expedition began in St. Louis, Missouri. About

---

1. **Purchase** : acquisition.

The Lewis and Clark Expedition

50 men travelled up the Missouri River. They explored the territory and made maps.

After six months they stopped and built Fort Mandan. They spent the long winter there.

In the spring of 1805 the expedition continued. An Indian woman called Sacagawea went on the expedition with the explorers. She was a friendly Shoshone Indian.

Sacagawea spoke English and other Indian languages. She was very helpful. Sacagawea's brother was a Shoshone chief. A Shoshone guide helped the explorers cross the high mountains. The journey was difficult and dangerous. Grizzly bears[1] and other animals attacked the explorers.

The explorers built canoes. They travelled down

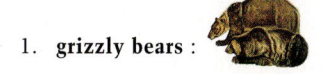

1. **grizzly bears** :

The American West

the Columbia River to the Pacific Ocean! They arrived at the Pacific Ocean in November 1805. They built a fort there.

The expedition returned to Missouri in September 1806. The explorers travelled 8,000 miles (12,800 kilometres) from May 1804 to September 1806.

The Lewis and Clark expedition was very successful. Lewis and Clark made many maps. They brought back a lot of information about the West.

In the 1840's John Fremont and Kit Carson explored the land between the Rocky Mountains and the Pacific Ocean. They visited California and Oregon. Fremont made the first scientific map of the West.

Another important pioneer was Davy Crockett. He fought for the independence of Texas.

This was the beginning of the great movement to the West.

The expedition spent the winter at Fort Mandan.

UNDERSTANDING THE TEXT

1 Choose the correct word and circle it.

a. In 1803 President Thomas Jefferson *bought* / *sold* the Louisiana territory for $15 million.

b. In 1804 Lewis and Clark went to *live in* / *explore* the Louisiana Purchase.

c. About *fifteen* / *fifty* men travelled *up* / *down* the Missouri River.

d. They spent the *winter* / *year* in Fort Mandan.

e. Sacagawea was a friendly Shoshone Indian *chief* / *woman*.

f. In 1805 the Lewis and Clark expedition arrived at the Pacific *River* / *Ocean*.

g. John Fremont and Kit Carson were two important *explorers* / *Indians*.

2 Match the adjectives with the correct situation.

e.g. When you see your friend you are happy.

SITUATIONS

a. When you run a lot
b. When the summer holiday ends
c. When you go to the library
d. When you want to drink
e. When you want to eat
f. When you see a grizzly bear

ADJECTIVES

1. you are thirsty
2. you are frightened
3. you are hungry
4. you are sad
5. you are tired
6. you are quiet

3 Descriptions

Look at these characters. Use the words in the canoe to describe them.

M. Lewis and W. Clark   Sacagawea

....
....
....
....

canoe words: courageous   friendly   helpful   explorers   made maps   built a fort   Indian   spoke many Indian languages

CHAPTER FOUR

Let's go West!

After the Lewis and Clark expedition settlers, gold prospectors [1] and trappers [2] went to the West. The American frontier was immense.

Settlers wanted to build homes and farms in the West. They wanted a better life. Gold prospectors wanted to find gold and become rich. Trappers wanted to hunt wild animals. This was an exciting period.

In 1841 thousands of pioneers began their long journey. They started in Independence, Missouri. From there they took the Oregon Trail or the Santa Fe Trail. (see map on page 28) They travelled for four to six months.

Most journeys began in the spring. The pioneers wanted to arrive before winter. The pioneers travelled in covered wagons

---

1. **gold prospectors** : people who look for gold.
2. **trappers** : people who hunt animals and then sell their skins.

The long wagon train. "The Jerkline" by Charles M. Russell, 1912.

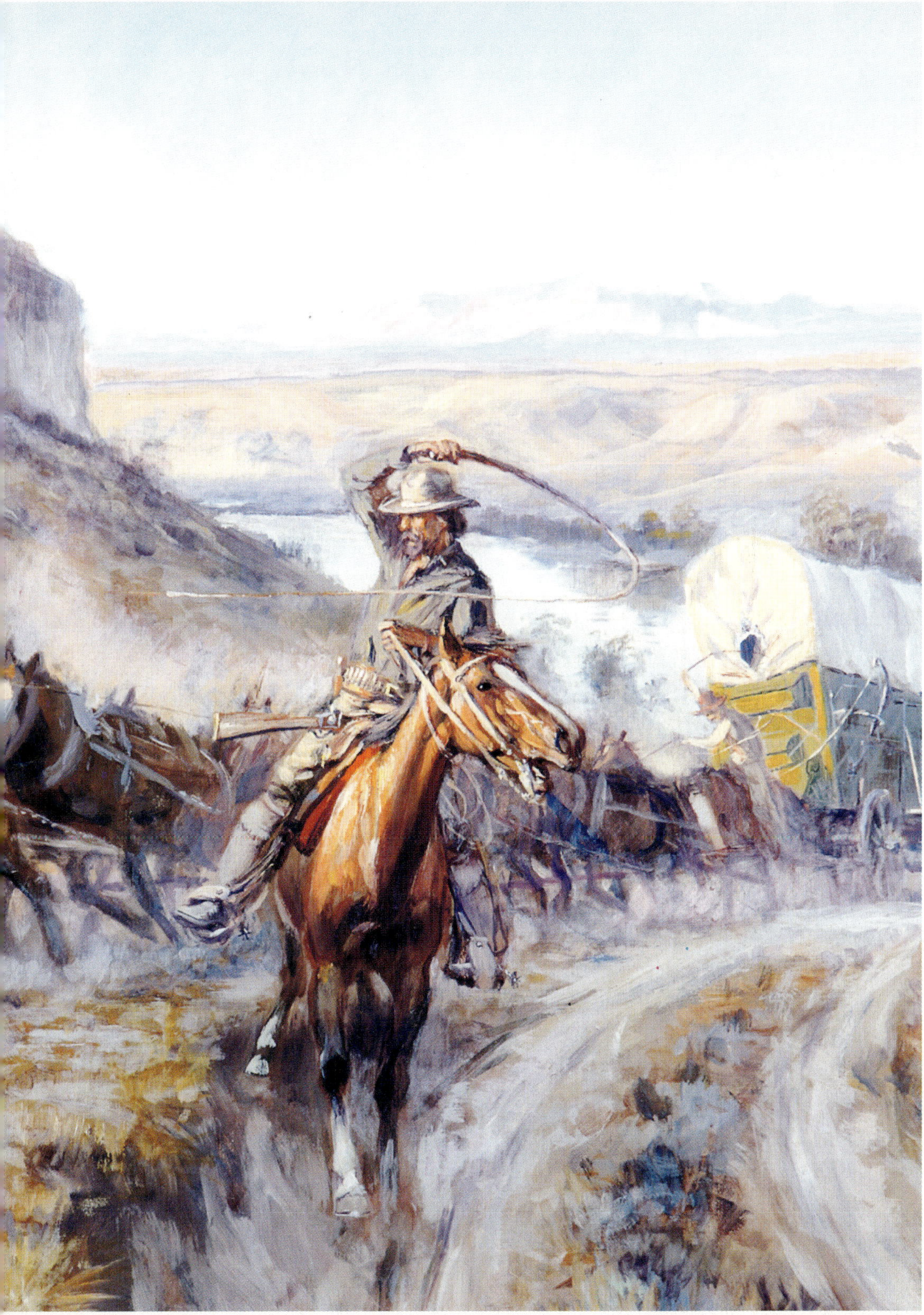

The American West

pulled by mules [1] or oxen. [2] They put food, clothes, furniture and other things in the covered wagon. A lot of families took cattle and sheep.

Many covered wagons travelled together. This was called a wagon train. All the wagon trains had a leader called a captain. They also had a scout. The scout knew the trail well. He walked in front of the others to look for Indians or other dangers.

The journey was long, difficult and dangerous. It was difficult to cross big rivers and tall mountains.

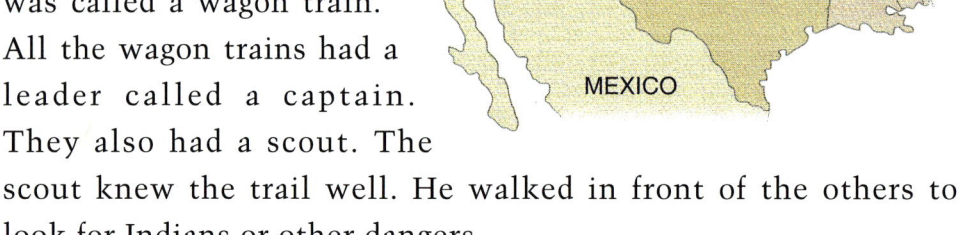

The weather was another problem. In the summer it was very hot. There was little water to drink. There was little grass for the animals to eat. Rain and snow were also a problem.

About 10,000 people died on the Oregon Trail between 1835 and 1845. The Indians killed only 400 people!

1. **mules**:

2. **oxen** (singular: ox):

Let's go West!

A Typical Day on the Trail:

5 a.m.: The pioneers got up and had breakfast. Then they began to travel.

Midday: The pioneers and the animals rested. They drank water and ate.

2 p.m.: The wagon trains began to travel again.

Sunset:[1] At sunset the scout chose a campsite. The wagon train made a big circle to protect everyone from wild animals. In the centre of the circle there were campfires.[2]

The pioneers sat around the campfires to eat and talk. They went to bed early because they were tired. A day on the trail wasn't easy!

A pioneer and his cattle.
"The Stampede" by Frederic Remington, 1910.

1. **sunset :**
2. **campfires :**

UNDERSTANDING THE TEXT

1. Choose the correct answer.

a. After the Lewis and Clark expedition many people
- [ ] crossed the Appalachian Mountains
- [ ] settled in Independence, Missouri
- [x] went to the West

b. The pioneers travelled for
- [x] four to six months
- [ ] one year
- [ ] about 6 weeks

c. The pioneers put food, clothes and furniture
- [ ] on fast horses
- [x] in the covered wagon
- [ ] on two mules

d. All the wagon trains had
- [x] a captain and a scout
- [ ] twenty covered wagons
- [ ] a doctor

e. In the summer
- [ ] wagon trains did not travel
- [x] there was little water to drink
- [ ] the animals ate a lot of grass

f. Between 1835 and 1845 on the Oregon Trail,
- [ ] there were many Indians
- [ ] the Indians killed 10,000 people
- [x] about 10,000 people died

2 *What, when, where, who, why*
Fill in the gaps with the correct *wh* word.

a. ...When... did the pioneers get up?

They pioneers got up *at 5 a.m.*

b. ...What... did the pioneers and the animals do at midday?

The pioneers and the animals *rested* at midday.

c. ...Who... chose the campsite?

The scout chose the campsite.

d. ...Why... did the wagon train make a big circle?

The wagon train made a big circle *to protect everyone from wild animals.*

e. ...Where... did the settlers sit to eat and talk?

The settlers sat *around the campfires* to eat and talk.

3 **Fill in the gaps with the prepositions that you find in the arrow.**

> between · by · on · after · in · before

a. Many people went to the West ...after... the Lewis and Clark expedition.

b. Thousands of pioneers travelled ...on... the Oregon Trail.

c. The pioneers wanted to arrive ...before... winter.

d. The settlers travelled ...in... covered wagons.

e. The covered wagons were pulled ...by... mules or oxen.

f. More than 10,000 people died on the Oregon Trail ...between... 1835 and 1845.

4 Have fun with this crossword puzzle!

ACROSS

1. 
2. 
3. a very hot season
4. 
5. this person looks for gold
6. this person hunts animals and sells their skins
7. something to eat
8.

DOWN

9. this person knows the trail well
10. a very cold season
11. name of an important trail
12. 
13. something to drink
14.

1. CAMPFIRE
2. MULE
3. SUMMER
4. RRACK / ROADS
5. GOLDPROSPECTOR
6. TRAPPERS
7. FOOD
8. MOUNTAINS

10. WINTER
11. OREGON
12. SUNSET
13. WATER
14. WAGON

32

5 Look at these illustrations and unscramble the words to write the names of the seasons. Then choose the correct words about each season. You will find the words in the covered wagon.

NPIRGS

MRUMSE

------

warm   hot
cold   cool   snow   ice
sunny   leaves fall
flowers begin to grow
people go on holiday
people go skiing

NTMUAU

TRWENI

CHAPTER FIVE

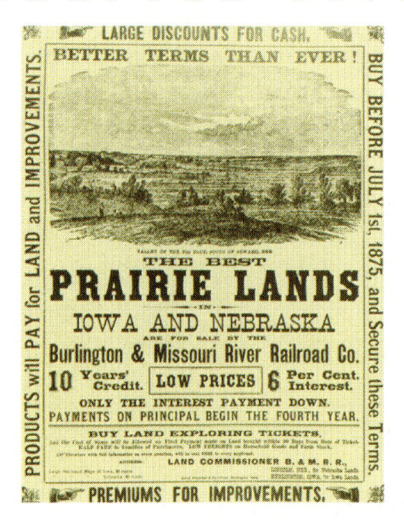

Life on the Frontier

When the settlers arrived at their destination they began to work. They began to build a home and plant crops. The home was usually made of logs.[1] It was called a log cabin. It was a small home with one or two rooms. The settlers made the furniture. They used logs to make tables, chairs and beds.

Men, women and children planted crops. Corn and wheat[2] were important crops. The settlers ate a lot of corn. The men hunted buffalo and other animals. Men, women and children worked all day. There was little free time.

There were no shops on the frontier. The settlers bought some things from Fort Laramie and Fort Bridger. Some women brought

1. **logs** :

2. **wheat** :

Frontier people were true American free spirits.
(U.S. Library of Congress.)

Abilene, a frontier town in 1879.
(Kansas State Historical Society, Topeka, Kansas.)

The American West

a spinning wheel [1] to the frontier. These women made yarn. [2] They used yarn to make clothes.

Illness was a big danger on the frontier. There were no hospitals, few doctors and very little medicine! Many people died at a young age.

Most settlers lived far from churches. When they wanted to get married, they waited for the "circuit rider". The "circuit rider" was a religious man. He travelled on the frontier. Settlers often waited months for the "circuit rider".

Who were the frontier people? The frontier people came from the East, the South and the Indiana Territory. They also came from Europe, Scandinavia and China! Most settlers were honest people but some were outlaws. [3] Some of them wanted excitement and adventure.

Frontier people were strong and courageous. They loved the freedom and adventure of the frontier. They were true American free spirits.

Villages and towns began to grow on the frontier. Some became important cities.

1. **spinning wheel** :
2. **yarn** :
3. **outlaws** : (here) criminals.

Pioneers used logs to build homes.

UNDERSTANDING THE TEXT

1 **Are these sentences true (T) or false (F)? Correct the false sentences.**

	T	F
a. When the settlers arrived at their destination they began to build a home.	☐	☐
b. The home was called a fort.	☐	☐
c. Corn and bread were important crops.	☐	☐
d. The settlers bought some things from Fort Laramie and Fort Bridger.	☐	☐
e. Not many people died at a young age.	☐	☐
f. Most settlers lived far from churches.	☐	☐
g. The frontier people were strong and courageous.	☐	☐

Frontier people loved freedom and adventure.

2 **Look at this sentence from Chapter 5:**

The home was *usually* made of logs.

Usually **is an adverb of frequency. We use adverbs of frequency to say how often something happens.**

Look at the frequency adverbs below. Then say what you do in your free time by putting the phrases under the correct adverbs. You will find the phrases in the old map.

listen to music
watch TV   read a book
meet friends   visit my grandparents
eat a pizza   play a musical instrument   sleep
phone a friend   go to the cinema
play football   listen to the radio
go to the disco   go shopping

always

....
....
....
....

usually

....
....
....
....

sometimes

....
....
....
....

never

....
....
....
....

3 You are a young settler. You and your family travelled on the Oregon Trail. Now you are in the Oregon Territory.
You want to write a letter to your best friend in Kentucky. Use the words in the envelope to complete the sentences.

> water   corn   hours
> animals   five   mother
> wagon train   fort
> log cabin   hot

Dear Tom,

I travelled on the Oregon Trail for .... months. My .... was attacked by the Indians. I was very frightened. It was very .... on the trail. There was little .... to drink.
My father built a .... My .... makes yarn on the spinning wheel. My brother and I planted ....
Yesterday we went to the .... to buy some things. We travelled for five .... We saw many wild ....

   Your friend,

4 Listen to the first five paragraphs of Chapter 5 and put the pictures in the order that they are mentioned.
Write 1, 2, 3 etc. in the correct box.

a. ☐

b. ☐

c. ☐

d. ☐

e. ☐

f. ☐

OUTLAWS OF THE WEST

It was very difficult to keep law and order [1] in the West. Most settlers were honest people, but there were a lot of outlaws. Outlaws robbed banks, trains and stagecoaches. Honest people were afraid to travel. There were horse thieves [2] and cattle thieves, but there were few sheriffs! Who were the sheriffs of the West? The most famous were Wyatt Earp, Pat Garrett, Wild Bill Hickock and Bat Masterson. Wyatt Earp and his brother Virgil were Western heroes. In October 1881 they killed three outlaws at the O.K. Corral in Arizona. The gunfight at the O.K. Corral became a legend. There are several films about this gunfight.

Who were the outlaws of the West? There were a lot of outlaws in the West. The most famous were Billy the Kid and Jesse James.

The O.K. Corral in Tombstone, Arizona.

1. **law and order** : respect for Government rules.
2. **thieves** (singular: thief) : people who steal; robbers.

Billy the Kid was a killer and a cattle thief. He worked on a cattle ranch in New Mexico. There was a $5,000 reward [1] for Billy the Kid. In 1880 Sheriff Pat Garrett captured him and put him in prison. Billy escaped from prison. He killed two of the sheriff's men. Sheriff Pat Garrett followed him to Fort Sumner, New Mexico.

On July 14 1881, he killed Billy the Kid during a gunfight. Billy was only 21 years old!

Jesse James and his brother Frank were bank and train robbers. They terrorised the West for many years. In 1881 there was a $10,000 reward for the arrest of Jesse or Frank James. On April 3 1882, an outlaw called Bob Ford killed Jesse in Missouri.

In the West horse thieves, cattle thieves and killers were usually hanged [2] when they were captured. The West was a violent place!

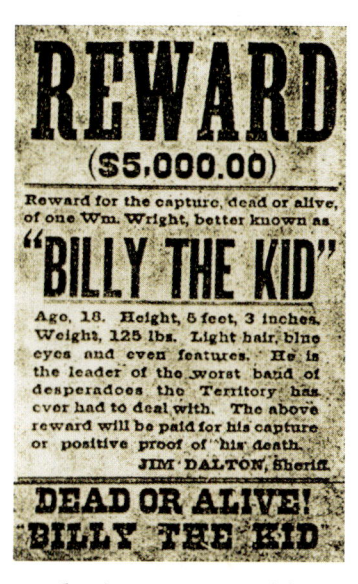

The $5,000 reward for Billy the Kid.

The sheriffs of the West, 1890. (U.S. National Archives.)

1. **reward** : (here) money given to someone for helping the sheriff to find a criminal.
2. **hanged** :

1 **Choose the correct answer.**

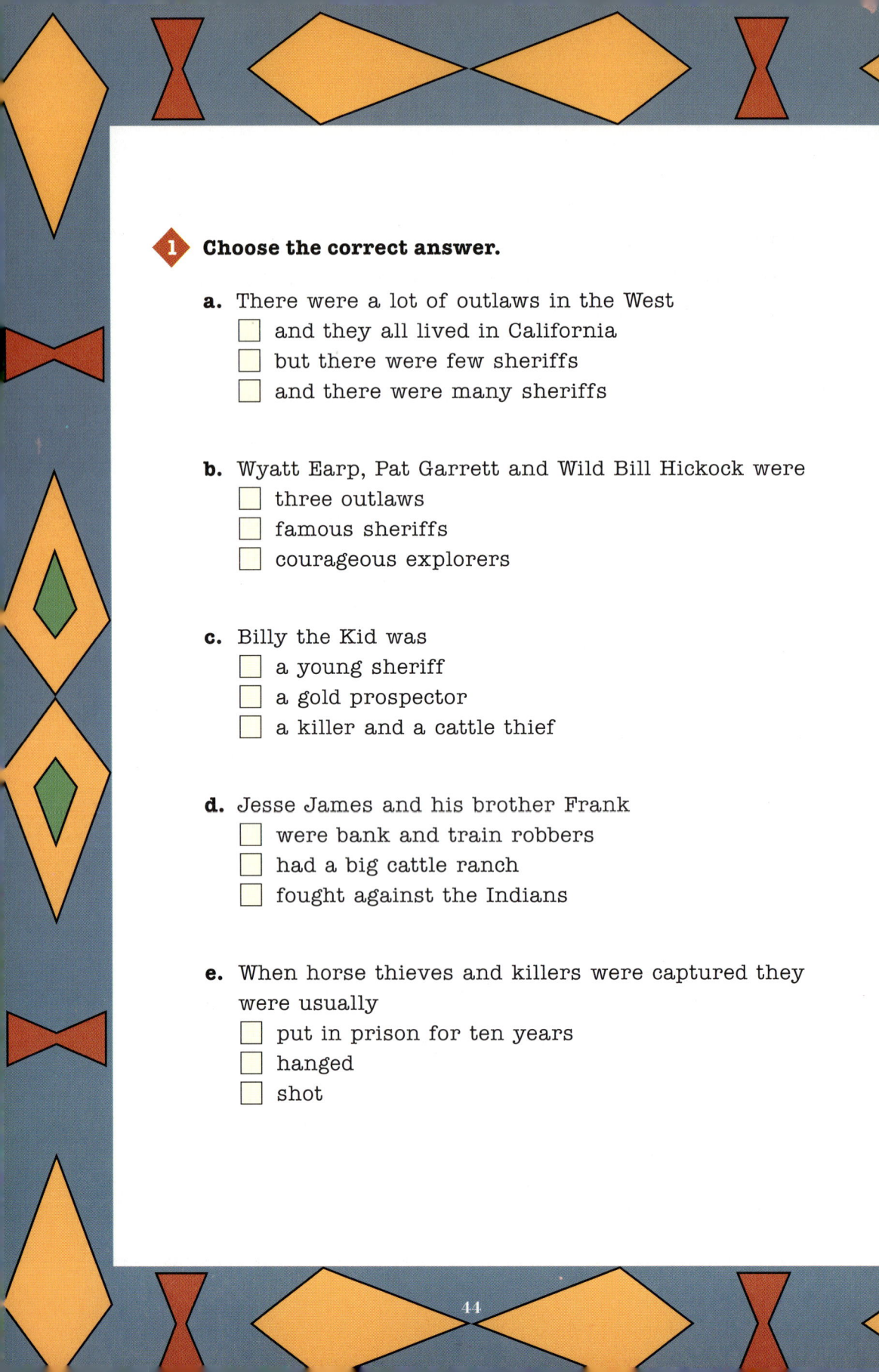

a. There were a lot of outlaws in the West
- [ ] and they all lived in California
- [ ] but there were few sheriffs
- [ ] and there were many sheriffs

b. Wyatt Earp, Pat Garrett and Wild Bill Hickock were
- [ ] three outlaws
- [ ] famous sheriffs
- [ ] courageous explorers

c. Billy the Kid was
- [ ] a young sheriff
- [ ] a gold prospector
- [ ] a killer and a cattle thief

d. Jesse James and his brother Frank
- [ ] were bank and train robbers
- [ ] had a big cattle ranch
- [ ] fought against the Indians

e. When horse thieves and killers were captured they were usually
- [ ] put in prison for ten years
- [ ] hanged
- [ ] shot

2 **Identify the outlaws!**

How much do you know about the outlaws of the West? Complete their identities.

Name	.... the	.... James
Description	Killer and	Bank and ....
Reward	$	$ ....
Killed by	....	....
Year	....	....
Place	....	....

3 How many words with three or more letters can you make with this title?

THE AMERICAN WEST

Two are done for you.

tea ....
can ....
....
....

CHAPTER SIX

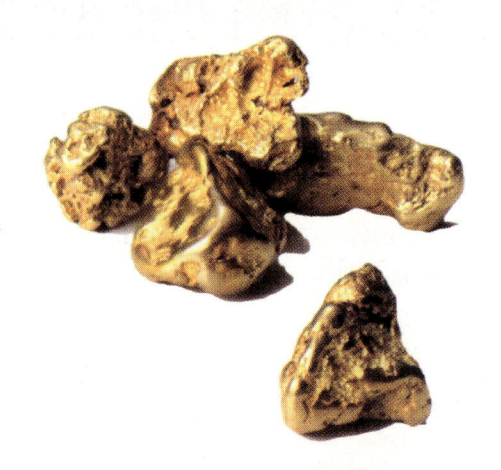

The California Gold Rush

In 1848 John Marshall discovered gold at Sutter's Fort in California. This western territory became famous. Thousands of people travelled to California to look for gold. This was the California gold rush. These people were called "Forty-Niners".

The first "Forty-Niners" arrived in San Francisco in February 1849 on the steamship *California*. Others came to California on the Oregon and California Trail. In 1849 almost 100,000 people arrived in California to look for gold! San Francisco became a very important city.

There were many small mining towns in the California Gold Country. Many "Forty-Niners" found gold, but only some of them became rich and important.

The California Gold Rush

A map of California's gold mining towns.

The discovery of gold changed the destiny of California and the West. The population of California grew very quickly. It became the 31st state of the United States in 1850.

A lot of people travelled to the West. A lot of gold travelled from California to the East. From 1852 the Wells Fargo stagecoaches travelled from the East Coast to the West Coast. Wells Fargo was a very important company in the West. The stagecoaches carried passengers, money, mail and gold across the continent.

A journey across America by stagecoach was a great adventure!

Four or six horses pulled the Wells Fargo stagecoaches. There were four to six passengers in every stagecoach. The

"Forty-Niners".

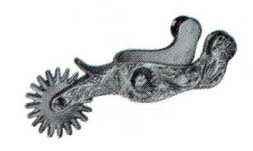

The American West

journey was very uncomfortable. The stagecoaches travelled all day and all night. Passengers slept inside the coaches on hard seats. Indians and outlaws attacked the stagecoaches.

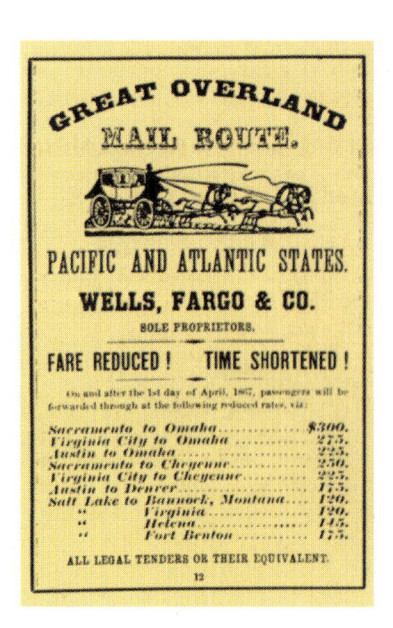

A Wells Fargo stagecoach.

A Wells Fargo office in the 1890's.

UNDERSTANDING THE TEXT

1 Fill in the gaps with the correct words from the stagecoach.

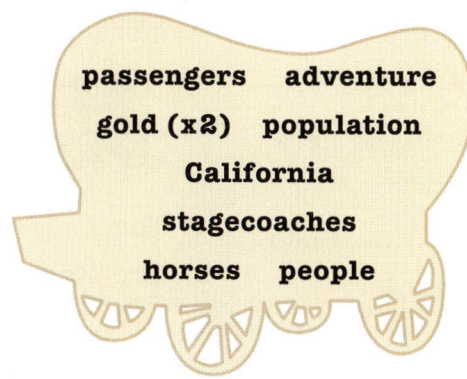

> passengers   adventure
> gold (x2)   population
> California
> stagecoaches
> horses   people

a. In 1848 John Marshall discovered .... at Sutter's Fort .

b. Thousands of people travelled to .... to look for ....

c. In 1849 almost 100,000 .... arrived in California.

d. The .... of California grew very quickly.

e. The Wells Fargo .... travelled across America.

f. Stagecoaches carried ...., money, mail and gold.

g. A journey by stagecoach was a great .... !

h. Four or six .... pulled the stagecoaches.

2 Unscramble these sentences.

a. California / were / many / in / towns / mining / there.
b. gold / "Forty-Niners" / found / many.
c. rich / became / important / and / some.
d. carried / money / stagecoaches / passengers / and.
e. was / the / uncomfortable / journey / very.
f. the / attacked / Indians / stagecoaches / outlaws / and.

3 **Have fun with this Western crossword puzzle!**

ACROSS

1.
2. gold was discovered here
3. famous trail
4. The California .... Rush
5. A very important American city

DOWN

6. Important company in the West
7.
8. The .... looked for gold
9. The stagecoaches carried this
10.

4 Listen to the first two paragraphs of Chapter 6. Then listen to them again and fill in the gaps.

In 1848 John Marshall discovered .... at Sutter's Fort in California. This western territory became famous. Thousands of people travelled to .... to look for gold. This was the California gold rush. These people were .... "Forty-Niners".

The first "Forty-Niners" .... in San Francisco in February 1849 on the steamship *California*. Others .... to California on the Oregon and California Trail. In 1849 almost 100,000 .... arrived in California to .... for gold! San Francisco became a very important ....

Many "Forty-Niners" found gold.

5 **A Western town**

Match the following and then label the town.

a. you keep your money
b. you eat, drink and play cards
c. you buy food, clothes and other things
d. you pay to sleep
e. horses and mules eat and sleep

1. in a hotel
2. in a stable
3. in a bank
4. in a shop
5. in a saloon

S _ L _ _ _ _

B _ _ _

_ _ T _ _ _

_ H _ _ _

_ T _ B _ _ _

COWBOYS!

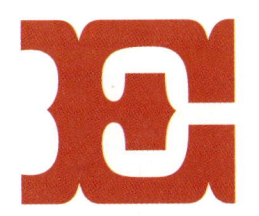

Everyone knows the word "cowboy"! The cowboy is an important part of American folklore. There are many films about cowboys and the West. The cowboys were young, adventurous men. Many cowboys were white, but others were Mexicans or Afro-Americans. The cowboy's life was difficult. Cowboys followed a severe code of conduct. They lived in difficult conditions. They worked from morning to evening. Often they worked at night, too.

Cowboys rode horses and looked after cattle. "When Cowboys Get in Trouble" by Charles M. Russell, 1899.

Cowboys worked on a ranch. They rode horses and looked after cattle, day and night. They moved the cattle from one grazing place [1] to another.

Cowboys took the cattle to the nearest railroad station. This was often about 1,000 miles (1,600 km) away! It took many weeks to arrive. At the railroad station the cowboys sold the cattle. The cattle went by train to the East. Americans liked good meat from the West.

What did cowboys wear? A cowboy always wore a big hat. It protected him from the hot sun and the rain. He wore a bandana [2] around his neck. He used the bandana to protect his

Cowboys at a saloon in Colorado, 1875.
(U.S. Library of Congress.)

1. **grazing place** : where cattle eat grass and drink water.
2. **bandana** :

nose and mouth. He wore a shirt, a vest[1] and trousers. Every cowboy wore big boots and had a pistol.

There are still cowboys in the United States today! They work on cattle ranches in the West and they ride horses.

Cowboys at work.

1. **vest** :

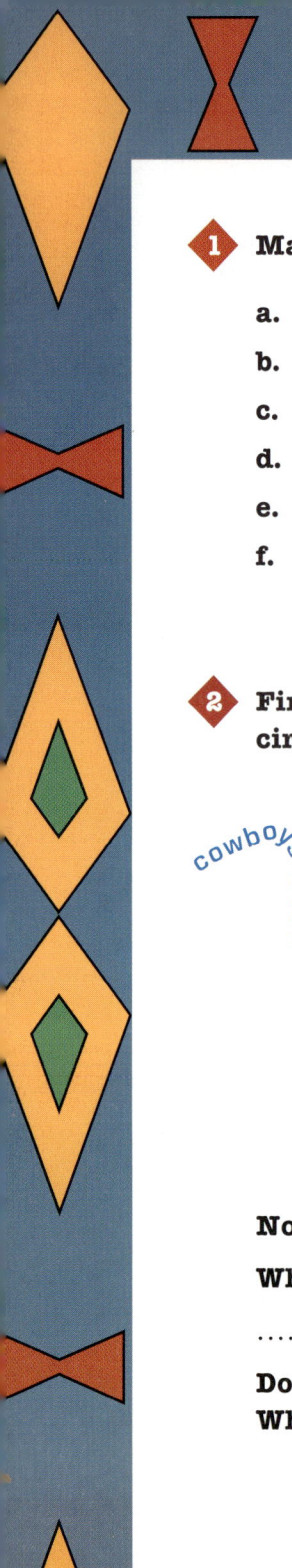

1 **Match the following:**

a. Cowboys were
b. The cowboy's life
c. Cowboys rode horses and
d. Cowboys took the cattle
e. At the railroad station,
f. In the U.S. today

1. looked after cattle
2. the cowboys sold the cattle
3. to the nearest railroad station
4. young, adventurous men
5. cowboys work on cattle ranches
6. was difficult

2 **Find six pieces of a cowboy's clothing in this word river and circle them in red.**

cowboyshatshirtwerevestsstrongbootscourageoustrousersmenbandana

Now underline the other words in black.

What sentence do you get?

....

**Do you agree with this sentence?
Why or why not?**

"The Cowboy" by Frederic Remington, 1902.

CHAPTER SEVEN

The Indian Wars

The Indian Wars began in the 1800's. Thousands of pioneers went to the West. They took the Indians' land. The Indians were angry. They did not want to lose their land.

The Wars of the Midwest

In 1811 the Shawnee Indians of the Indiana Territory attacked the settlers and the U.S. Army.

These Indian wars continued until 1832. The Black Hawk War was the last Indian war in the Midwest. The Indians lost this war and their land.

The Wars of the South-East

In the 1830's Osceola was the chief of the Seminole Indians of Florida. He said, "We will fight until the last drop of Seminole blood!" The Seminole Indians did not want to leave their land.

The Indian Wars

They fought for many years. In 1837 Chief Osceola was captured. Most of the Seminoles were killed.

The Cherokee Indians were a strong and important tribe. They had big plantations [1] and farms. The settlers wanted their land. In 1839 the U.S. Government told the Cherokees to leave their homes. They went to an Indian reservation in Oklahoma. Many Indians died during the long journey. The journey was called the Trail of Tears. [2]

The Wars of the Great Plains

In the 1850's many pioneers crossed the Great Plains. Many of them settled there. The Sioux and Cheyenne Indians fought against these settlers.

The Sioux and Cheyenne Indians were courageous warriors. The Sioux Chiefs were Crazy Horse, Red Cloud and Sitting Bull. They told their warriors, "Fight to kill, or you will lose your lands!"

The Sioux and Cheyenne Indians attacked U.S. Army forts and settlers. The fighting was terrible. It continued for many years.

1. **plantations** : big pieces of land where cotton, sugar and tobacco are cultivated.
2. **Tears** :

The American West

The U.S. Government told the Indians to go to an Indian reservation. Chiefs Crazy Horse and Sitting Bull did not want to go. There were a lot of brutal battles. Many people were killed.

The Apache and Comanche Indians also fought against the U.S. Army and the settlers for many years.

"The Massacre of Sand Creek, Colorado Territory" by Robert Lindneux.

The Indian Wars

The Apaches were great warriors. They loved their land and their freedom. They didn't want to lose them. They preferred to fight and die. Geronimo and Cochise were famous Apache chiefs. Their courage was legendary. Everyone was afraid of Geronimo and Cochise. The Indian Wars ended in 1890.

UNDERSTANDING THE TEXT

1 **Choose the correct answer.**

a. The Indian Wars
- [ ] ended in the 1850's
- [ ] began in the 1800's
- [ ] began in the 1700's

b. The Indians were angry because
- [ ] the pioneers took their land
- [ ] they didn't have any rifles
- [ ] they didn't have any food

c. In the 1830's Osceola was
- [ ] a scout
- [ ] a friendly Indian woman
- [ ] the chief of the Seminole Indians

d. The Cherokee Indians
- [ ] had big plantations and farms
- [ ] lived in the Midwest
- [ ] were a small tribe

e. The Sioux and Cheyenne Indians
- [ ] lived in California
- [ ] were friendly
- [ ] were courageous warriors

f. The Apache and Comanche Indians
- [ ] fought against the U.S. Army
- [ ] did not fight in the Indian Wars
- [ ] lived in Florida

2 **Look at the map of the United States and fill in the names of the tribes in the correct places.**

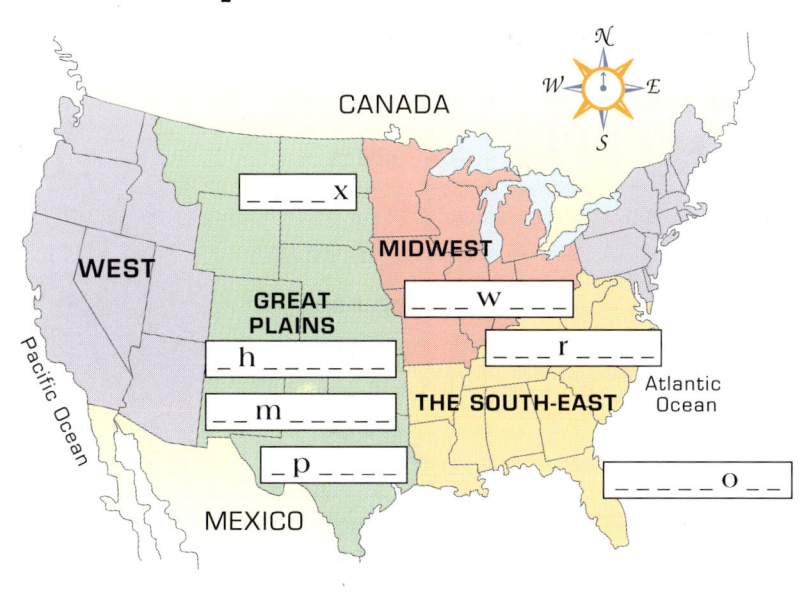

_ _ _ _ x
_ _ _ w _ _ _
_ _ _ r _ _ _ _
_ h _ _ _ _ _ _
_ m _ _ _ _ _
_ p _ _ _ _
_ _ _ _ _ o _ _

3 **Let's make a short summary of Chapter 7. Fill in the gaps with the correct words from the log.**

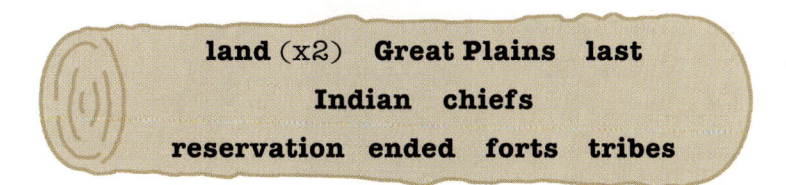

> land (x2)   Great Plains   last
> Indian   chiefs
> reservation   ended   forts   tribes

The .... Wars began in the 1800's. Thousands of pioneers went to the West and took the Indians' .... There were many wars. The Black Hawk War was the .... Indian war in the Midwest.

The Seminole and Cherokee were important .... They lost their .... and went to live on a .... in Oklahoma.

The Sioux and Cheyenne Indians lived on the .... They attacked U.S. Army .... and settlers.

Geronimo and Cochise were great Apache .... The Indian Wars .... in 1890.

4 Label the cowboy

Can you name the cowboy's clothes? Write the words from the cowboy hat in the correct places on the picture below.

shirt
hat   boots
vest   bandana
trousers

_ _ _

_ _ _ _ _ _ _

_ _ _ _ _ _ _

_ _ _ _ _ _ _ _

_ _ _ _

_ _ _ _ _